Whoever you are right now is exactly the right person to take you in to the next stage of life.

You've never been in a better position to begin your journey towards your goals!

Everything that's happened up until now has been preparation for your future, even if you can't see how yet.

So start now, start where you are, start with what you have. Just start. And go out there and do great things!

1

HOW TO USE THIS BOOK

This book is designed to be both read and written on.

There are 52 passages opposite a blank page with the intention that you use one every week, as a journal prompt or as support for your inner guidance.

You can use them in order, or you can use them randomly.

Some may speak to you more at different points in your life, so if you don't feel resonance with one you can flick through and find one that works for you that week.

Use the blank page in whatever way feels most like you. Write, draw, scribble, do nothing...

I hope that some of these words offer the same support and motivation to you as they have done for me x

You Got This

NEVER SAY NEVER

You CAN do that crazy thing you wanna do.

You CAN achieve the mad goals that you dream about.

You ARE capable.

No more doubts OK - whatever it is you want - get up and go after it.

YOU GOT THIS!

AIM ABOVE YOUR TARGET

Goal setting often goes like this - you aim for what you know you can achieve, you work hard, do what you have to do and you reach your goal. Yay!

But what if you could actually achieve more?

By aiming higher than feels comfortable, and pushing beyond the limits you THINK you have, you can set new standards of achievement that may surprise and amaze you!

CREATE A RELATIONSHIP WITH YOURSELF

Do you have a real and true relationship with yourself? Enough that you can sit in silence with yourself without reaching for your phone or wanting to connect with a friend?

So many of us are always messaging others, always responding to what is happening, or telling the story of our experience. And that pulls us away from the absolute wonder of what is here right now, in front of us.

When you have a relationship with yourself so that you feel secure and loved, that is when you can let go of the need for others around you all the time. You can be in silence. You can appreciate the world. You can be whole. You can be in love with life.

You can have it all.

NO ONE IS MOTIVATED ALL THE TIME

It is perfectly normal to lose motivation. It is also normal to want to take a break from the one thing you said you would always care about.

Life goes up and down, motivation goes up and down, passion goes up and down.

But the one thing that doesn't is your commitment to yourself.

So don't wait for your motivation to come back. Accept now for what it is and decide what to do, using your commitment to yourself as a guide.

When you do that the motivation will come back.

DON'T STAY DOWN

Learning and growth always involve some element of failure. Just the very act of trying to achieve something will immediately put you at risk of NOT achieving it.

So you WILL fall down, or be knocked down. You wouldn't be human if that didn't happen.

But you don't have to stay down.

You don't have to be defeated.

Failure is not defeat.

So when you find yourself knocked down, don't stay down. It is not your final destination.

Get up, keep going, move forward, enjoy the journey, rise again.

YOU CAN'T SAY THE WRONG THING TO THE RIGHT PERSON

And you can't say the right thing to the wrong person.

So don't spend your energy worrying about what has been said. That is done, that is in the past.

Or, for that matter, worrying about what you should say in the future.

The right person will see you for who you are anyway, and if someone sees you in a negative light then let them.

You can't take responsibility for other people's thoughts and actions and you can't blame yourself for them.

16

FIND HAPPINESS WITHIN

Happiness isn't what you have or your status in life.

Happiness isn't something you chase through goal setting.

True happiness comes from within, no matter what the outside circumstances are.

When you find happiness within yourself you will have peace of mind and security, rather than constantly looking to chase the next achievement.

Not only that, your failures and disappointments will also carry less meaning, and you will have a strong and harmonious base from which to live your life.

THIS IS YOUR LIFE

(not anyone else's)

If you could live your life exactly as you please how would you live it differently?

And why is it that you don't live it exactly as you please?

This IS your life, this IS your journey and you have every right live it YOUR way x

You got this!

EMBRACE THE UNEXPECTED

Every path you find yourself on will take unexpected twists, turns, or complete changes of course.

It can feel scary and out of control.

It can feel annoying.

It can test our willpower and motivation to stay on track.

However the truth is that unexpected challenges are going to happen, and ultimately, these opportunities allow us to learn and to grow.

Stop resisting change. Allow yourself to embrace the unexpected.

BE PATIENT WITH YOURSELF

You don't always have to be on top form, flying high and crushing it. Sometimes your body and mind won't be in tune. Sometimes you just don't feel right. Sometimes you are unwell.

There could be so many reasons why things aren't happening as fast as you would like. But that's OK. There's no rush.

Be patient with yourself.

SELF LOVE OVER SELF IMPROVEMENT

Do you find yourself in a constant drive to improve and grow, without stopping to appreciate who you are right now?

If you do, you could be missing out on the greatest love in the world - the one you have for yourself.

Self love can be cultivated now. Without the need for improvement, or growth, or change.

Self love can be unconditional, forever love.

And when you have that for yourself you attract those who wish to love you on that level too.

GIVE WITHOUT EXPECTATION

Give for the feeling you get when you give, without expecting anything in return.

Watch how this allows you to appreciate yourself, your life and your relationships so much more.

Other people cannot be held accountable for what they do, and anyway it's not your job to make anyone feel any kind of way.

It's only your job to do that for yourself. So give, and feel good about it no matter what the reaction.

Giving to others without expectation is actually giving to yourself the gift of freedom.

28

CONSISTENCY IS KEY

Results don't come from one or two weeks of action, if they did then we would all be walking around with everything we ever wanted.

Results come from sustained action, over the long term.

You must be prepared to take the same action over and over.

You must be committed.

Consistency is key when it comes to reaching your goals.

DO MORE OF WHAT YOU LOVE

Bring more of what you love into your world by doing more of what makes you happy.

For example if you love to be creative , how can you bring this pleasure into your world right now? Could you bring creativity into the way you move your body?

If you feel at home in the great outdoors what is a way to spend more time outside? Even if it is as small as a few minutes every day, perhaps with your bare feet on the ground.

Look for the possibilities, look for the openings, look at what you can do.

Look and see how you can do more of what you love x

MAKE THE MOMENTS COUNT

We don't always remember the big things in life - so often what we remember is only a moment.

Just one small part of a day.

That one moment could stay in your brain as a memory, creating happy thoughts for years to come.

So if we can make the moments count then our memories will be filled with beauty, joy, love and connection.

CREATE SPACE FOR YOURSELF

Space is created by removing what you don't need.

Physically discard what you no longer require, or is not useful.

Keep only that which enriches your life.

Mentally clear out any clutter.

Keep only those thoughts which lift you up or lead you forward.

Spiritually create space for you, to be yourself, to thrive and to grow.

Create space for yourself to feel nurtured, to feel safe.

UNLOCK YOUR POTENTIAL

Unlocking your potential starts with knowing and accepting who you are, so that you can use the gifts you were born with to create success.

What can you do this week to get to know yourself a bit better?

What can you do to get closer to unlocking the full potential of YOU

GO THE EXTRA MILE

You can choose how much work you put in to a task.

You can choose how much time you give to a relationship.

You can choose how much effort you put in at work.

You always have a choice.

So do you choose to do just enough, or do you choose to do more?

Choose to go the extra mile, and watch as your experience of life grows.

TAKE YOUR OWN ADVICE

Isn't it curious that we can worry and stress for days over problems, seemingly not knowing what to do, but someone else could have the same issue and we could offer some words of wisdom immediately.

You are a fantastic source of advice for others, why not for yourself!

Next time you have a problem, issue or question, ask yourself for some advice...

And then take that advice.

Problem solved!

FREE YOURSELF FROM JUDGEMENT

Our harshest critic is often our own mind. Who else would judge us the way we do?

We judge our bodies, the things we spend money on, our achievements, our relationships and our lifestyle choices.

But have you stopped to wonder what anyone else would say? Do you believe another human would really be as harsh as you can be?

Would another person disregard all the positives the way you do?

No! Other people see you for who you are - a beautiful human.

Because you are.

So free yourself from judgement. Free your mind, free your time, free your soul. And then go forward being unapologetically YOU.

TRUST THE PROCESS

There are times when it can feel like life is going off in the wrong direction.

Maybe you feel like you made a wrong decision, and now you can't imagine how things will work out the way you originally planned.

But let's stop for a moment to remember that it doesn't mean life is wrong, or that you are wrong.

Life has never followed a straight path for anyone. Everyone successful has a few stories of where it all seemed to go wrong.

So trust the process of life. It's a journey of ups and downs. There is good and there is bad.

And yet somehow things are always working out.

REFUSE TO BE AVERAGE

Average is not for you.

No - you are more than that.

If you were to settle for being average then you would be letting yourself down.

Also think of what gifts you would be denying the world.

It's not your place to be average - refuse it at all costs!

ONE DAY AT A TIME

Success doesn't happen all at once - it happens as a result of lots of tiny positive actions.

What matters is the little things you do every day.

Stay positive, and take one day at a time.

Sooner or later you will look back and realise how far you've come.

LIFE IS A MIRACLE

Have you ever stopped to think about your body?

About the heart that beats, all day and all night.

About the skin which protects everything inside, so much so that it heals itself when it is sliced open.

About the way that you take food and drink in to your body and it is converted in to energy.

Or the way the signals from your brain can tell your body to move.

When you stop to consider your body and what it does, it's hard to choose any other word to describe it other than a miracle.

So next time you find yourself being disappointed in yourself in some way, remind yourself that being alive is a mad, special, incredible privilege.

EVERY END IS A NEW BEGINNING

It can be really sad when a good thing comes to an end. You may experience heartbreak and devastation, you may feel really lost and really low.

But the end is never just the end.

It's always a beginning too.

THE TRUTH WILL SET YOU FREE

The truth may not be the easiest path, it could be inconvenient and in some cases it may be very a difficult path to take.

But it is the path which will ultimately lead to freedom, power, love and all the good stuff in life.

Free yourself from the trap of lying.

Free yourself from the downward pull of not knowing the truth.

The truth will set you free, open you up and give you the life you deserve.

TREAT YOURSELF AS A FRIEND

When you are talking to yourself do you talk the way you would talk with a friend?

Do you treat yourself with respect and compassion?

Next time you feel yourself having negative inward chatter, stop for a moment, run over it in words - as if you were saying it out loud to a friend. Listen to those words, really listen. Then ask yourself if you would treat a friend like that.

And if the answer is no, then you need to stop treating yourself like that.

Just stop.

You are worth so much more and you deserve respect from yourself as much as anyone.

THE ONLY WAY TO GET OVER THE FEAR OF DOING IT, IS JUST TO DO IT

We have all been there - afraid to do something new for fear of what might happen.

And thats's ok.

But there is a way to get over the fear.

And that is just to do what you are afraid of.

So go out there and do the thing!

DEFY EXPECTATIONS

Expectations are not real, they are opinions.

When have you ever let opinions hold you back?

Defy the expectations of others and of yourself. Be amazing!

Go above and beyond what is expected of you.

Go on DO IT.

LET INSPIRATION DRIVE YOU

The things that inspire you are important.

Not only do they put a spring in your step and give you an emotional boost, they also give you clues about what matters to you.

So when inspiration strikes, follow it.

Act on it.

See how it can drive you to create a life you love and feel AMAZING!

What inspires YOU?

YOU ALREADY KNOW THE ANSWER

Do you ever feel yourself struggling to decide what to do, and not knowing the answer?

So much time can be wasted going over and over what is right, and what is wrong, and what might happen if.... And that just is not helpful, especially when you already know the answer.

Yes you do.

Take some time alone, let your mind be free from distractions, and pay attention to where it goes.

Think of the emotions you are feeling, think about what they are saying to you, explore if those emotions have meaning.

You DO know the answer, you DO know what's best for you 🤍

DARE TO BE DIFFERENT

Stand up! Be brave. Be bold. Be you!

You influence the world by being you, no one else is quite like you.

And because you are unique you, the world wants your biggest and best contributions.

Be your wild and different self, go on, dare ya!

REJECTION IS A NORMAL PART OF LIFE'S JOURNEY

Not everything is going to be right for you. Not every job you apply for will be a good fit, not every person you like will like you back.

You will not glide through life without rejection of some kind.

And that is a good thing.

Rejection is part of the process of weeding out what is good for you and what is not meant for you. It saves you from having to always be the one to make the hard decisions.

When you are rejected that decision is made for you and you have the opportunity to feel how you need to feel and then to move forward.

Celebrate all the rejections of your past for helping you to become who you are.

THIS IS A NEW WEEK

Today is a new day, the start of a new week.

A week filled with beautiful opportunities to feel all the ways you want to feel.

With every day this week remind yourself that each morning is a fresh start in life.

Within this new week there are 7 beautiful new days to appreciate all that you have and all that you are.

WHY HOLD BACK

Give me one good reason to hold yourself back from the opportunities that exist in the big wide world.

I am going to the a bet that at the base of that reason is fear.

 what are you afraid of?

Not getting it "right"? Having to start again? People laughing at you?

How about flipping it on its head and thinking of all the things that could go right, all the people you might meet, the growth you could have, the experiences awaiting you...

Why hold back from all that there is, and all that YOU could become!

REGRET NOTHING

Regret uses up energy and time, and in return gives only sad feelings.

Regret also takes attention away from the present moment, which in turn takes away any joy.

Therefore regret is an emotion with no benefits.

So love big, dream bigger, go hard, push further, go for it right now, be all you can be.

Without any regret.

BE BOLD

Stand up, be brave, be bold, go for it.

Go on - you know what a brilliant impact you could make!

Don't be shy. Take chances, put yourself out there, make waves.

You may believe that YOU are the only person who misses out by being afraid to stand out, but when you are bold we all win.

When you put your energy into the things you are most passionate about, you are able to give your biggest and best contribution. And the world NEEDS that!

Be courageous, be bold, be proud!

FIND STRENGTH IN THE STRUGGLE

Life will become hard at times, there WILL be struggle, that's just the way it is.

There is no life without struggle.

But the beauty of life is that it is in all your struggles that you learn more about yourself and you grow.

It is in the hard times that you develop.

So the struggle is not something to avoid, it is something to value.

GIVE OUT WHAT YOU WANT TO RECEIVE

It is not fair to expect to receive something in to your existence that you are unwilling to give.

What you want has to be something that you are prepared to give.

Imagine it like a friendship - you have to trust one another, they cannot trust you if you are not willing to trust them.

So what do you want to receive that you do not already have? How can you give this out, so that you can start the process of seeing it come back to you?

Give to get - love for love, truth for truth, joy for joy.

CHASE THE FEELING

If you won the lottery, what is the first thing you would buy?

Now ask yourself WHY?

When we break down our desires and plans for life it will always come down to one thing - the way we expect to FEEL when we get there. It may be happiness, security, joy, love... There is always a feeling at the base of what we want.

So instead of chasing the things, the job or the person, chase the feeling.

Bypass the first step and get straight to the good stuff.

APPRECIATE RIGHT NOW

Right now is the only thing we really have. The past is gone and the future is still to come.

So to appreciate right now is to appreciate everything.

Take a moment right here, right now, to look for something to enjoy, to savour, to love. There is always something, even is it is small, even if it is simple.

By using that as a point of focus watch how your mood can lift, your spirits can grow stronger, your love for life gets greater and you just feel better more of the time.

87

WORK ON YOU, FOR YOU

You are no one's project except your own.

Work on yourself for who you will become FOR YOU.

You are the one who has to spend every day of the rest of your life with you after all.

Might as well make it as enjoyable an experience as possible.

MAKE THE CHANGE

Change is scary sometimes, at other times it is exciting.

But the fact will always remain that doing something that frightens you could be the best decision you ever made!

And now is as good a time as any to make the change you need to make!

It's a great week to take the step.

Move forward.

Go on - you got this!

LEAD FROM THE HEART

You are the leader of your self, of your decisions, of your life.

How you choose to lead yourself affects more than just outcomes, it affects the way you experience the journey and ultimately how you feel about yourself and your life.

It would be wrong to suggest that this journey is always easy or that you always feel like it's going your way.

The truth is that there are ups and downs, lefts and rights, good times and bad. But through all of these you have the opportunity to lead with your heart.

And when you do, you find yourself on a path that is beautiful and wonderful and unique to you.

YOUR ATTENTION BELONGS ON YOUR OWN LIFE

While it is tempting to scroll the feed and give hours of attention looking at the perfect lives of others, that is not where your attention belongs.

It belongs on your own life, where you can make a difference.

You owe it to yourself to give your time, your energy and your love to **your own life**.

How can you bring your attention to where it needs to be this week?

THE BEST IS YET TO COME

The best days of your life are still to come. That is not to say that you have not already had amazing days. You have.

But if you don't believe that the best days are still to come then you will spend today living in the past. And what good will come of that?

The past is behind all of us, we can never get it back and we can never re-live it.

But what we can do is live in the time we have now and keep an open heart and an open mind for all the joy that is available in the future.

There will be incredible experiences in your future, let yourself feel excited about them!

YOU ARE A PRODUCT OF WHAT YOU REPEATEDLY DO

Not what you do once or twice a month, but what you do over and over again.

So you could have the very best intentions for yourself when you choose to do your workouts three times every week, but if you repeatedly slump at your desk and spend lunchtimes sitting staring into your phone, you will be a product of those often repeated lazy actions, rather than the inspired effort at the gym.

Your body and mind respond to what you do most often, over and over, on a daily basis.

So to change who you are and to change the results you are getting in your life - take a note of and change the little repetitive actions.

Because you are a product of what you repeatedly do, even if you don't mean to be.

FORTUNE FAVOURS THE BRAVE

Good fortune is no matter of luck alone.

Those who are prepared, ready and brave will have better luck than those who wait for things to come to them.

You always have the choice to be brave.

You have the choice to boldly step out towards what you want and need.

It's time to step out and step up, so that good fortune knows where to strike next.

COMPASSION OVER JUDGEMENT

"In a world where you can be anything, be kind."

Humans will judge, it is what we do. We are designed to make decisions about others based upon how they look and act. That is how we stay safe and how we align ourselves with the right people.

But ask yourself if your judgement of others is always kind. Because if it is not then are you really acting in a way that is best for you?

Who you judge another person harshly you will always be expecting other people to do the same to you. You will always worry about how you are perceived and what people are thinking about you. Negativity will seem natural and it just doesn't feel good.

Being kind to others, while seeing who they are or what they did, however, allows you complete freedom from worry about what others are thinking of you.

It also feels better to be kind

SELF LOVE IS NOT AN ACTION

For you self love may be to have a bath or go buy something special, for me it may be to take a walk and get outside with my dogs, for someone else it may be to take a week off and go somewhere with no phone coverage.

Just because one thing feels good for someone else does not mean it feels good for you. Self love is not in the actions, it is in the meaning that those actions have for you.

What does it mean for you to take a bath? Is it relaxing, does it give you space, does it make you feel special, is it part of your recovery?

What does being outside with my dogs mean for me? Is it relaxing, does it give me space, does it make me feel special, is it part of my recovery?

The meaning can be the same even tho the action is different. Because self love is not the actions. It is the meaning behind the actions, it is the way you feel before, during and after.

So don't look to others for ideas of how to love yourself, instead ask yourself how you want to feel and choose how to give yourself that.

YOU ARE MORE THAN ENOUGH

You know yourself better than anyone else, and often that means you are constantly able to see your 'faults' and where you feel you need to improve.

However, no one else creates stories about your faults and your weaknesses the way you do.

Perhaps by being so close to everything, you can't see the simple truth.

You can't see your greatness.

You can't see that you are more than enough.

BE WILLING TO FEEL WHAT YOU ARE FEELING

Don't worry if you are tired or drained. It's gonna happen sometimes. Especially at the end of the year.

We all get feelings that overwhelm us sometimes, but it's important to remember that without feelings you have no way to know yourself.

Strong feelings let you know that you care, and they help you to set your internal compass.

Being willing to feel all that you feel is going to help you to know all that you are; to move forward in the direction that's right for you.

So as you move out of this year, do so with courage and acceptance of everything you experience, and know that when you acknowledge all that you feel, you begin to really live in alignment with YOUR values and beliefs.

Printed in Great Britain
by Amazon